Understanding Science

Key Stage 2
Animals and Plants

Penny Johnson

Name _Uma Maheswary_

Schofield & Sims

Introduction

The Earth is home to millions of different animals and plants, and to micro-organisms so small that they can only be seen with a microscope. All these living things depend on each other for food and for a place to live.

In this learning workbook you will learn about how plants grow and reproduce. You will also learn about the different places where plants and animals live, and how animals feed. You will find out how things decay, and how micro-organisms can be useful.

How to use this book

Before you start using this book, write your name in the name box on the first page. Then decide how to begin. If you want a complete course to learn about animals and plants, you should work right through the book from beginning to end.

Another way to use the book is to dip into it when you want to find out about a particular topic. The Contents page or the index at the back of the book will help you to find the pages you need.

Whichever way you choose, don't try to do too much at once – it's better to work through the book in short bursts.

When you have found the topic you want to study, look out for these icons, which mark different parts of the text.

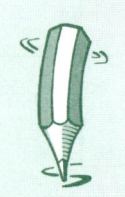

Activities

These are the activities that you should complete. You write your answers in the spaces. After you have worked through all the activities on the page, turn to pages 31 to 35 to check your answers. When you are sure that you understand the topic, put a tick in the box beside it on the Contents page.

Explanation

This text explains the topic and gives examples. Read it before you start the activities. Any words shown like **this** appear in the combined index and glossary. Look at page 36 to see what these words mean.

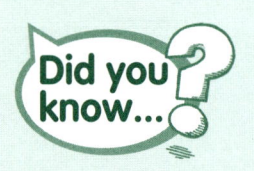

Information

This text gives you useful background information about the subject. Surprise your friends with some fascinating facts!

Contents

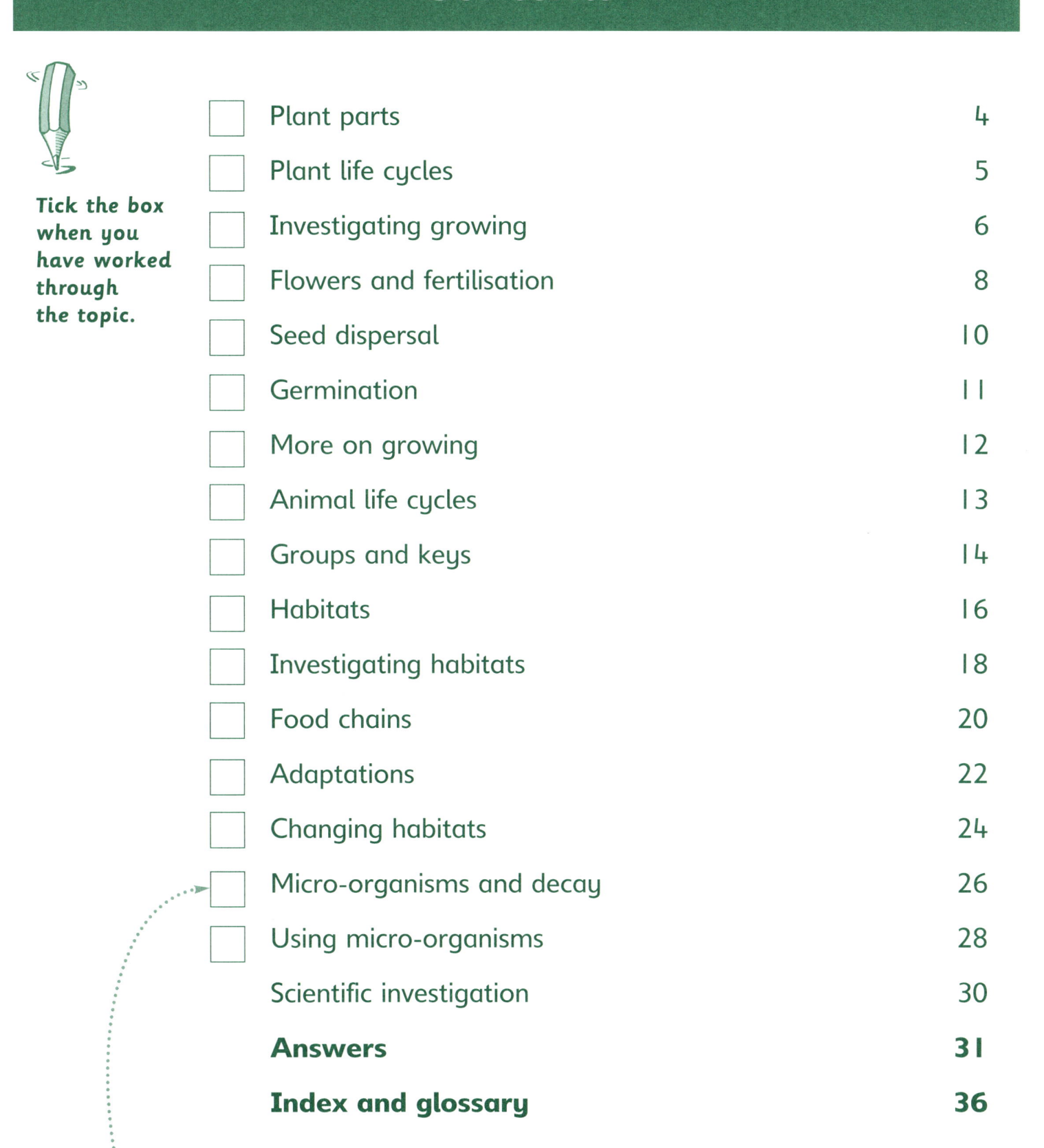

Tick the box when you have worked through the topic.

- [ ] Plant parts — 4
- [ ] Plant life cycles — 5
- [ ] Investigating growing — 6
- [ ] Flowers and fertilisation — 8
- [ ] Seed dispersal — 10
- [ ] Germination — 11
- [ ] More on growing — 12
- [ ] Animal life cycles — 13
- [ ] Groups and keys — 14
- [ ] Habitats — 16
- [ ] Investigating habitats — 18
- [ ] Food chains — 20
- [ ] Adaptations — 22
- [ ] Changing habitats — 24
- [ ] Micro-organisms and decay — 26
- [ ] Using micro-organisms — 28
- [ ] Scientific investigation — 30

Answers — 31

Index and glossary — 36

You will find out more about how micro-organisms can cause decay in the book **Our Bodies**, which is also in the **Understanding Science** series.

Plant parts

Plants are important because we need them for food, and so do other animals.

Plants have four main parts.

The flowers help the plant to **reproduce**.

The leaves make food for the plant. They need light, air, water and warmth.

The stem has little tubes inside it so water can travel from the roots to the leaves. The stem also supports the plant.

The roots take in water from the soil, and hold the plant in the soil.

1. Match up the parts of the plant with what they do. Some parts have more than one job.

roots	take in water
leaves	make food
stem	carries water to the leaves
flowers	hold the plant in the soil
	help the plant to reproduce
	supports the plant

2. Which three parts are important for helping the plant to grow?

_____

4 | Animals and Plants   Schofield & Sims | Understanding Science

Plant life cycles

The diagram shows how plants grow and reproduce. All the stages together are called the **life cycle** of the plant. You will learn more about the different stages on pages 8 to 11.

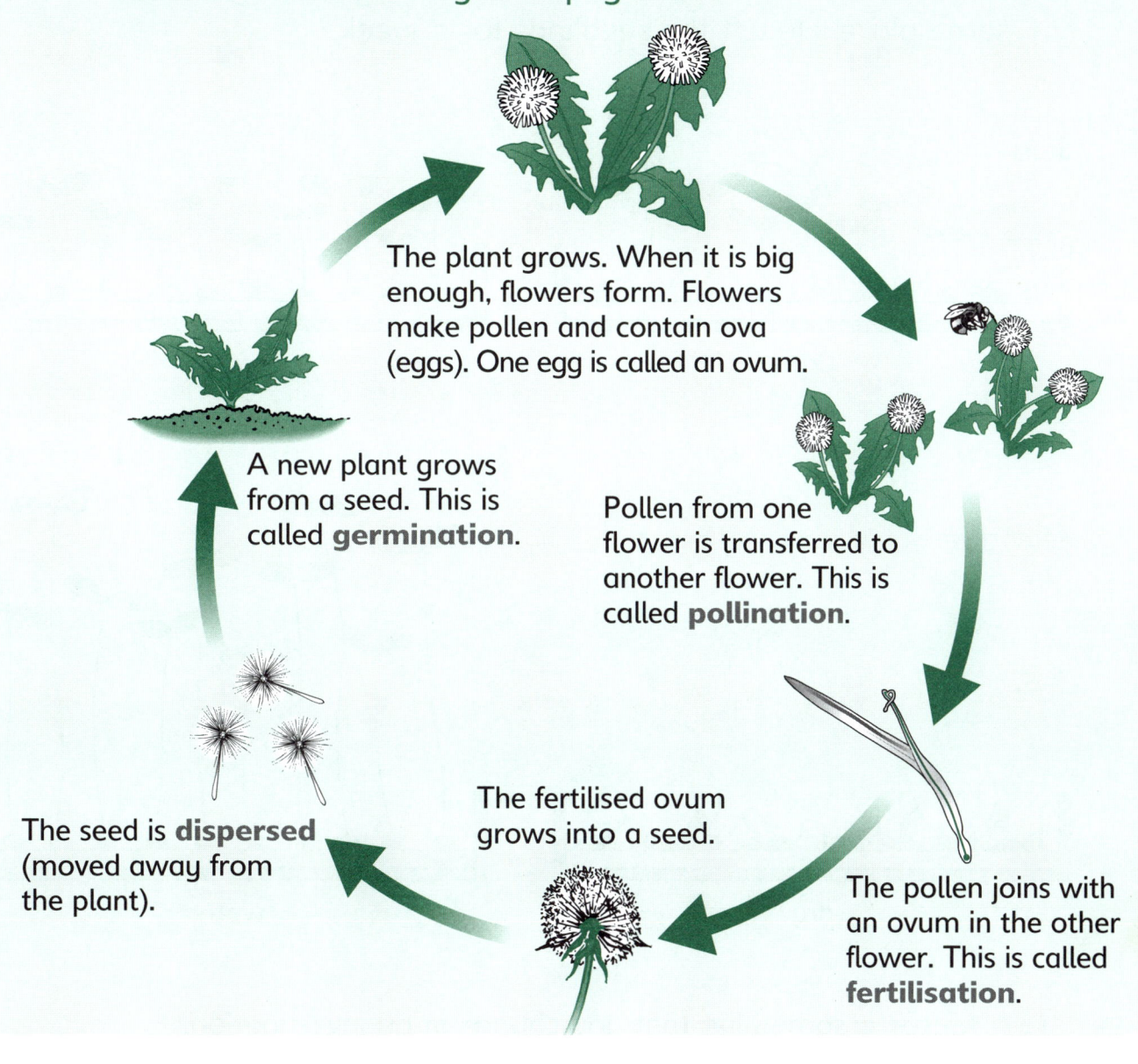

The plant grows. When it is big enough, flowers form. Flowers make pollen and contain ova (eggs). One egg is called an ovum.

A new plant grows from a seed. This is called **germination**.

Pollen from one flower is transferred to another flower. This is called **pollination**.

The fertilised ovum grows into a seed.

The seed is **dispersed** (moved away from the plant).

The pollen joins with an ovum in the other flower. This is called **fertilisation**.

1. Which two things join when fertilisation happens?

_____

2. Write these things in order to describe the life cycle of a plant.

| dispersal   fertilisation   flower formed   germination |
| ~~growth~~   pollination   seed formed |

_growth_____

_____

Understanding Science | Schofield & Sims   Animals and Plants **5**

Investigating growing

Liam is investigating the things that plants need to grow well. In his first investigation he used two dishes of cress seedlings with different amounts of water. He made his test fair by keeping them both in the same place. He left the seedlings for a week.

A

Start

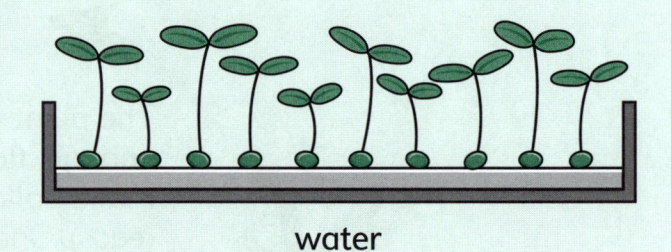

dry   water

After a week

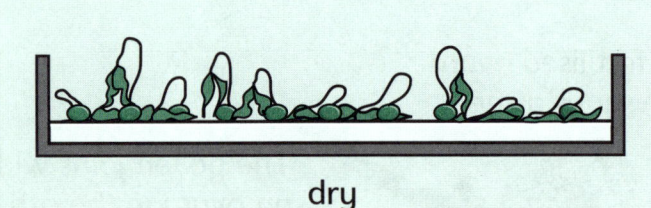

dry   water

1. A **factor** is something that you change in an investigation.

   a) Which factor did Liam change? _____

   b) Which factors did Liam keep the same?

   _____

2. A **conclusion** is what you find out from an experiment. Write a conclusion for Liam's investigation.

   _____

   _____

Investigating growing

An **evaluation** is when you decide how good your experiment was, and if it was a fair test.

> I think my results are reliable because I tested 10 seedlings in each dish, and all the seedlings were the same type. If I only used one it might have died anyway.

Liam set up two more investigations.

B
warm
a little water
light

warm
a little water
dark

C
warm
a little water
light

cold
a little water
light

These are the results of investigation B.

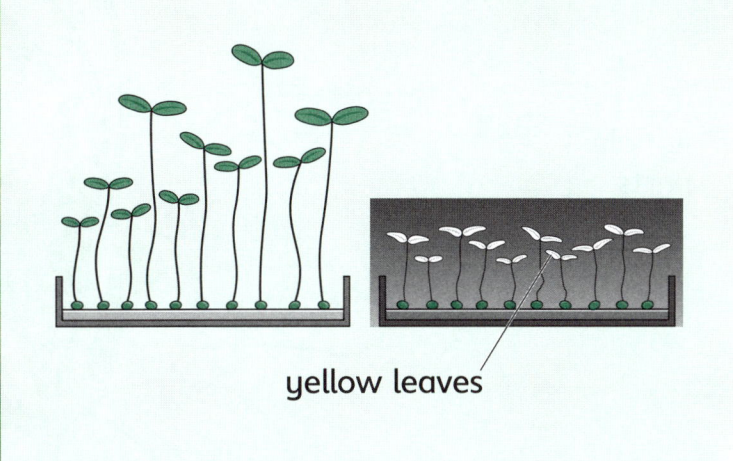

yellow leaves

3. How do the results of investigation B show that plants need light to grow?

_____

_____

4. Explain why investigation B was a fair test.

_____

5. Plants need warmth to grow. What results will Liam get for investigation C?

_____

_____

6. Write an evaluation for experiment C.

_____

_____

Understanding Science | Schofield & Sims   Animals and Plants   **7**

Flowers and fertilisation

Flowers have many different parts which they need to help them to **reproduce**.

The coloured petals attract insects.

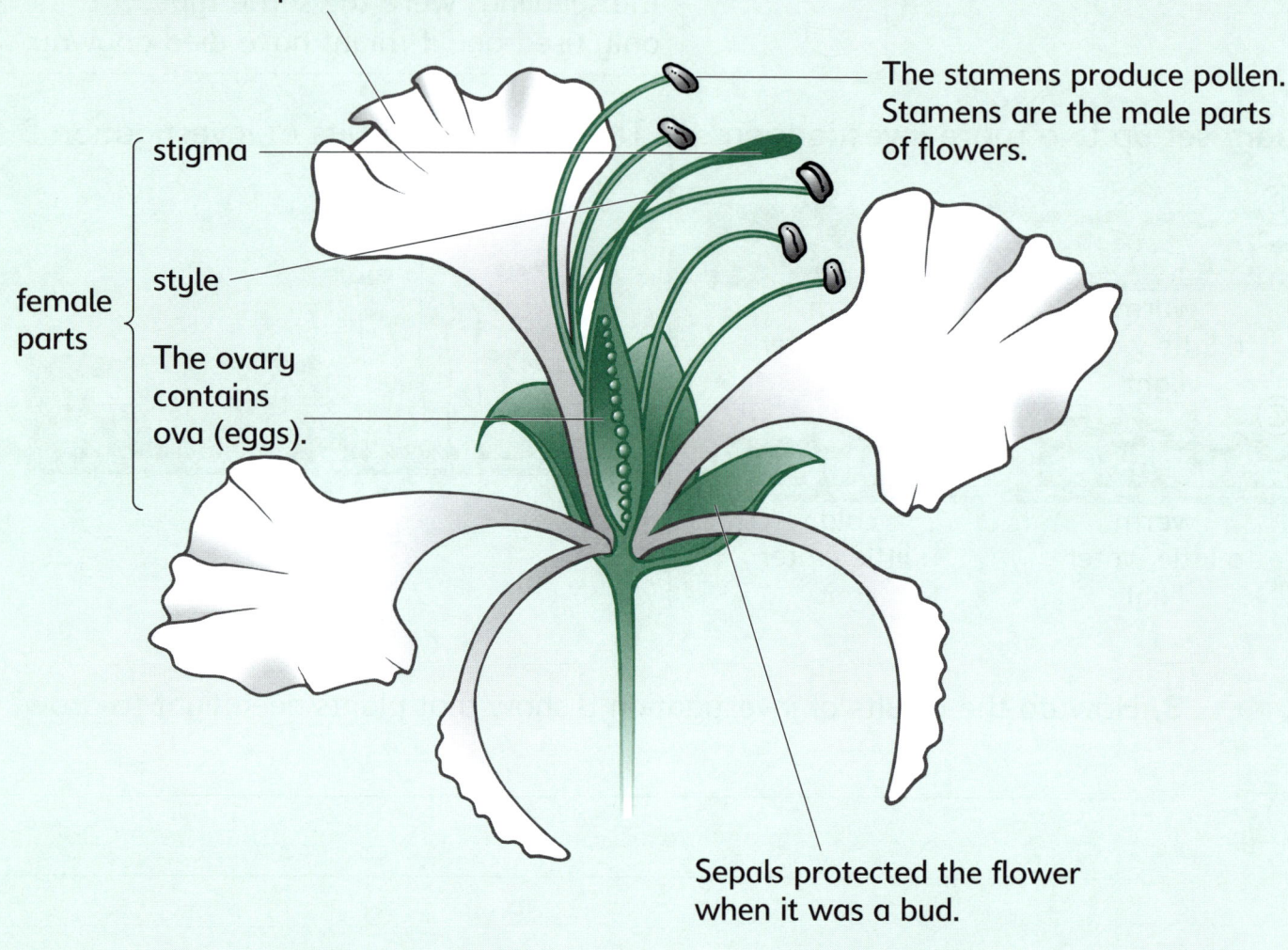

female parts
- stigma
- style
- The ovary contains ova (eggs).

The stamens produce pollen. Stamens are the male parts of flowers.

Sepals protected the flower when it was a bud.

Pollen from one flower has to be carried to another flower so that the plants can reproduce. This is called **pollination**. Flowers with brightly coloured petals are usually pollinated by insects. The insects come to drink a sweet liquid called nectar that the flower makes, and some pollen sticks to them. When they fly to another flower, the pollen may brush off onto the sticky stigma.

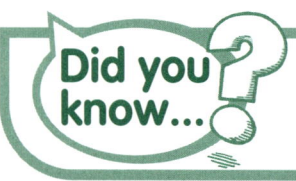

Did you know... Flowers also attract insects by smell. Most flowers with scent smell nice, but there are some flowers with a smell like rotting meat that attracts flies!

Flowers and fertilisation

Some plants have flowers that are very small and green. Pollen from these flowers gets blown by the wind onto other flowers.

When pollen lands on a stigma it starts to grow a tube down the style. The tube lets the pollen grain get to an ovum and join with it. This is called **fertilisation**. The fertilised ovum grows into a seed, and the ovary grows into a fruit.

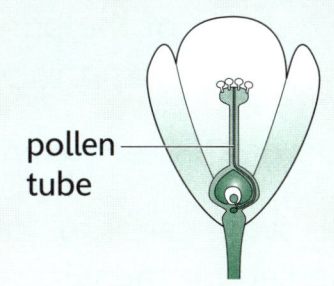

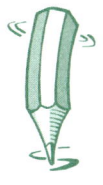

pollen tube

1. Write the correct parts of a flower in the boxes.

Parts of flower	What they do
	protect the petals when they are in a bud
	produce pollen
	attract insects
	grows into a fruit when the ovum has been fertilised
	sticky, so pollen grains stick to it
	grows into a seed when it has been fertilised

2. Why do flowers that are pollinated by insects have brightly coloured petals?

_____

3. Grass flowers are small and green. How do you think grass pollen is taken from one flower to another? _____

4. Put numbers next to these processes to show the order they happen.
   - [ ] The insect visits a different flower.
   - [ ] A tube grows down the stigma.
   - [1] The stamens make pollen.
   - [ ] An insect visits the flower to drink nectar, and some pollen sticks to it.
   - [ ] Pollen from the insect sticks to the stigma.
   - [ ] An ovum is fertilised and grows into a seed.

Seed dispersal

A seed can grow into a new plant. All plants need light, air and water to grow. If the seed just falls off the plant, it may be in the shade of the parent plant. It will grow better if it starts to grow away from the parent plant.

Seeds can be **dispersed** in different ways.

Light and fluffy seeds, or seeds with 'wings' are dispersed by the wind.

Animals disperse seeds. This can happen if seeds with hooks get caught on their fur. Animals also eat the fruit that grows around some seeds. The seeds pass through the animals and come out in their droppings.

Seeds can be dispersed by water (they get carried away by a river or stream). Some seeds are spread by explosions. These seeds grow in pods that split open and fling the seeds away.

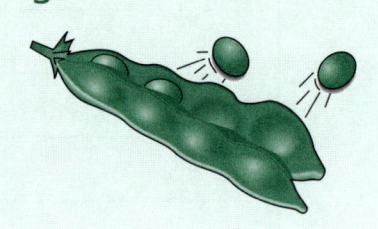

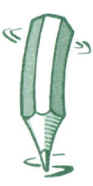

1. Why do seeds need to be dispersed?

   _____

2. a) How do you think this seed is dispersed?

   _____

   b) Write down one other way that animals can disperse seeds.

   _____

3. Groundsel has fluffy seeds.

   a) How do you think they are dispersed? _____

   b) Explain your answer to part **a)**.

   _____

Germination

Germination is when a seed starts to grow into a new plant. Seeds need water and warmth to germinate. They do not need light. Kerry wanted to find out what seeds need to germinate. She put some seeds onto a paper towel in 4 different dishes. The drawing shows what she did with each dish, and what her results were after 4 days.

Dish A — light, water, warm — After 4 days: seeds have sprouted on paper towel.

Dish B — light, no water, warm — After 4 days: no growth.

Dish C — light, water, cold — After 4 days: no growth.

Dish D — no light, water, warm — After 4 days: seeds have sprouted.

1. How does dish D show that seeds do not need light to germinate?

2. Which dish shows that seeds need water to germinate? _____

3. What does dish C show?

4. Why do you think Kerry needed dish A? _____

5. a) Do seeds need soil to germinate? _____

   b) Explain your answer.

6. Write down two things that seeds need to germinate.

More on growing

Most plants grow best if they are kept warm and have plenty of light and air, and enough water. Plants make their own food in their leaves using water, air and light.

Plants also need small amounts of other substances to grow well. Farmers add these **nutrients** to fields in fertilisers. At home, you might sometimes put 'plant food' onto a potted plant to keep it healthy. The nutrients in the fertiliser dissolve in water in the soil, and are taken into the plant through its roots.

Not all plants need the same conditions. Some plants are **adapted** to grow in different places.

Pondweed grows under water.

Cactus plants can grow in very dry conditions.

1. Which part of the plant makes food? _____

2. How does a plant get water? _____

3. What are nutrients?
   _____

4. How do nutrients get into a plant? _____

5. Julie says: 'Plants need lots of water.'

   a) Why is she partly right? _____
   _____

   b) Why is she partly wrong? _____
   _____

12 Animals and Plants   Schofield & Sims | Understanding Science

Animal life cycles

Animals are very small when they are born, and change as they get older. The changes that happen to an animal are called its **life cycle**. The drawing shows the human life cycle.

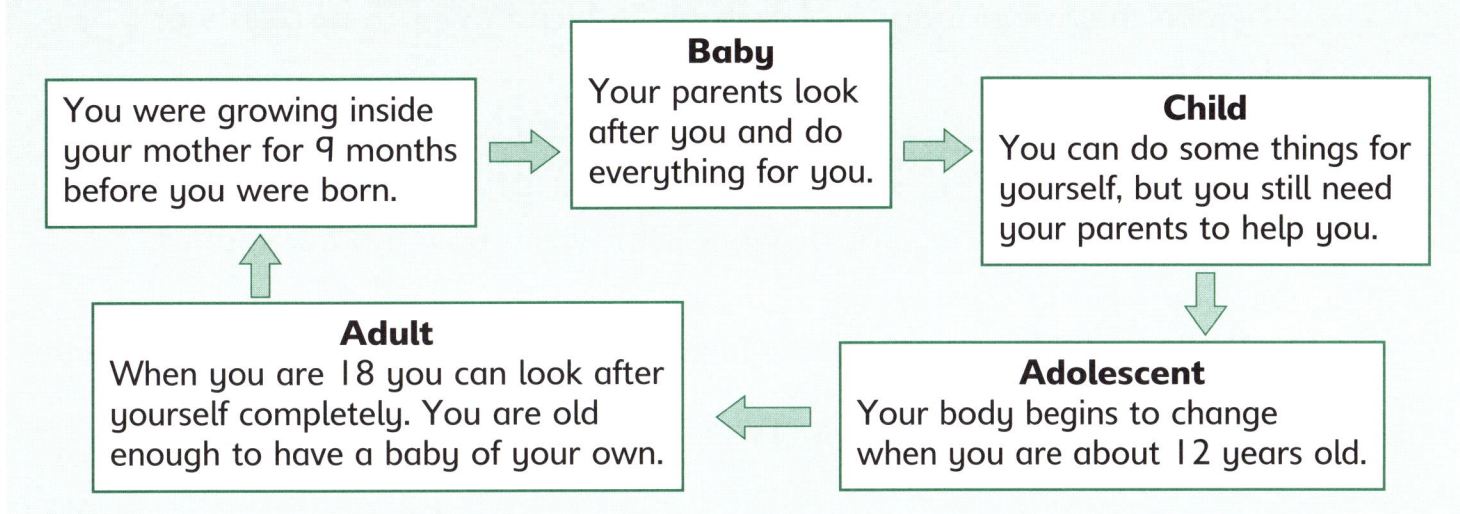

You were growing inside your mother for 9 months before you were born. → **Baby** Your parents look after you and do everything for you. → **Child** You can do some things for yourself, but you still need your parents to help you.

Adult When you are 18 you can look after yourself completely. You are old enough to have a baby of your own. ← **Adolescent** Your body begins to change when you are about 12 years old.

Humans need to be looked after for a long time after they are born. Other baby animals can look after themselves much sooner.

Kittens grow inside their mother for 65 days. They are ready to have babies of their own when they are about 1 year old.

A baby duck grows for a month inside an egg. It is ready to lay eggs of its own after a year.

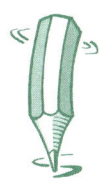

1. Write down two ways in which your parents look after you.

_____

2. What can you do for yourself that you could not do when you were a baby?

_____

3. Write down two differences between the life cycle of a duck and a human.

_____

_____

Groups and keys

An organism is a living thing. There are millions of different kinds of organism around us. It is easier to study **organisms** if we can put them into groups. Scientists divide organisms into plants (which make their own food) and animals (which have to eat plants or other animals).

These main groups are divided into smaller groups. Animals are divided into:
- **vertebrates** (such as humans or fish) which have backbones
- **invertebrates** (such as worms or woodlice) which have no backbones.

1. Birds have backbones. Tick two boxes to show which groups birds belong to.
   ☐ animal   ☐ plant   ☐ invertebrate   ☐ vertebrate.

2. A marestail makes its own food. Is it an animal or a plant? _____

Scientists need to be able to identify different animals and plants within these groups when they are studying them. Keys can help us to identify plants and animals.

A **key** has a set of questions which you answer as you work through it. The key below helps you to identify different birds you might see in a garden. The green line shows how you would use the key to find out that this bird is a wren:

brown wings and back

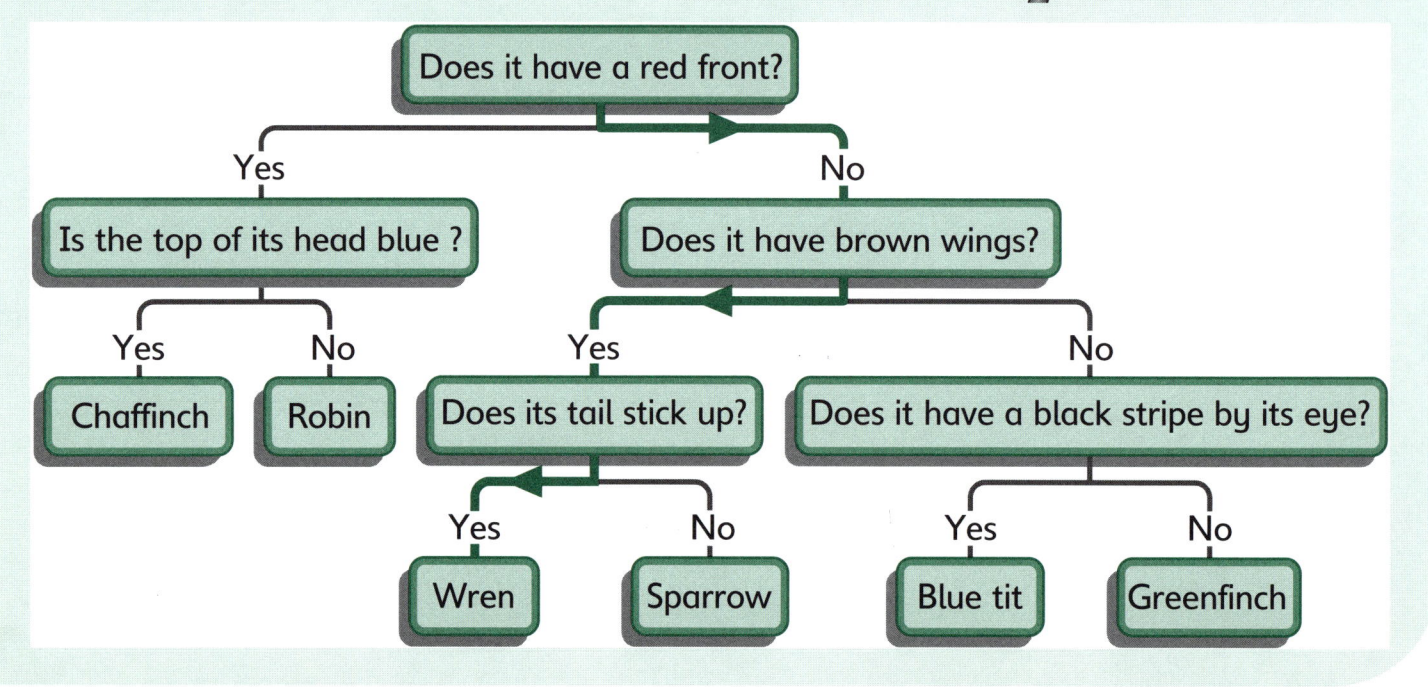

Does it have a red front?
- Yes → Is the top of its head blue?
  - Yes → Chaffinch
  - No → Robin
- No → Does it have brown wings?
  - Yes → Does its tail stick up?
    - Yes → Wren
    - No → Sparrow
  - No → Does it have a black stripe by its eye?
    - Yes → Blue tit
    - No → Greenfinch

Animals and Plants

Groups and keys

3. Here is the same key without the green lines. Use it to identify the birds below.

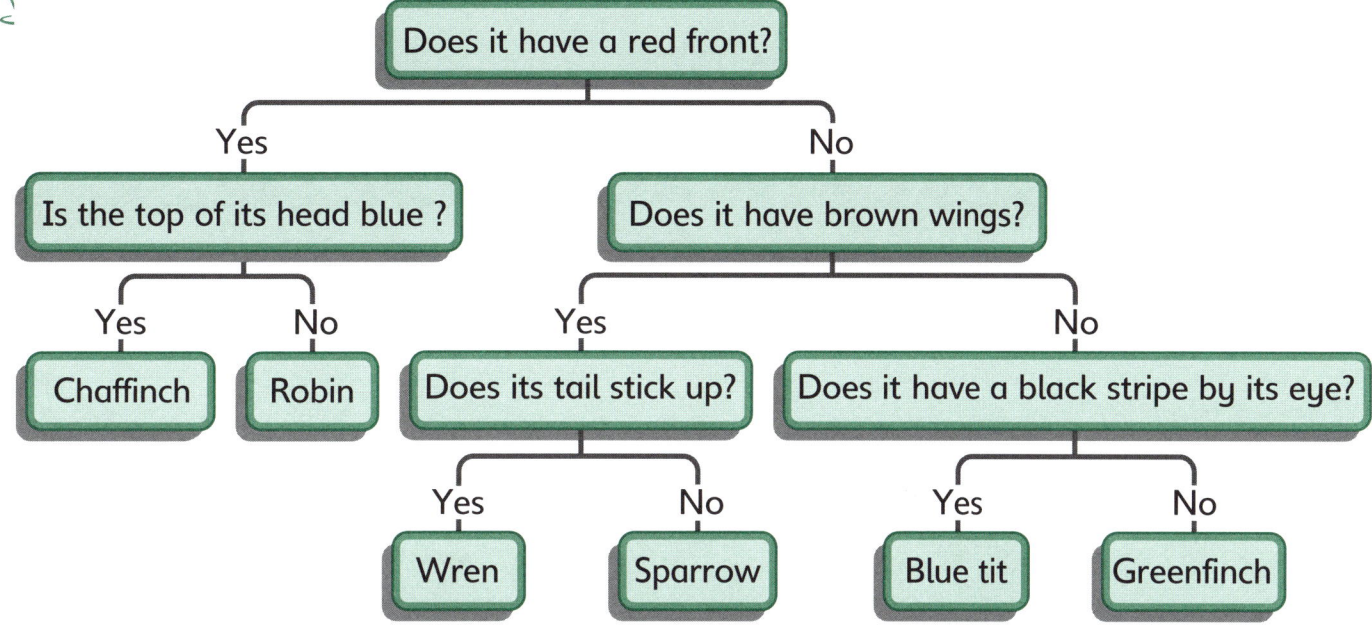

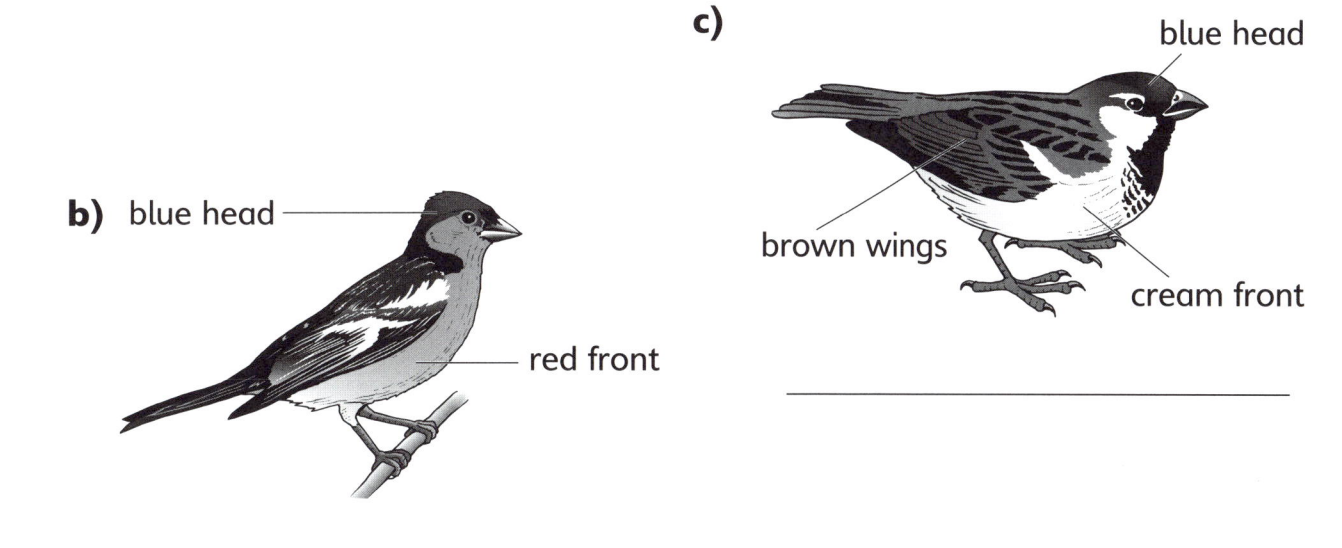

```
                    Does it have a red front?
                   /                          \
                 Yes                          No
                  |                            |
         Is the top of its head blue?    Does it have brown wings?
            /            \                 /              \
          Yes            No              Yes              No
           |              |               |                |
        Chaffinch       Robin      Does its tail stick up?   Does it have a black stripe by its eye?
                                    /            \              /              \
                                  Yes            No            Yes              No
                                   |              |             |                |
                                  Wren         Sparrow       Blue tit        Greenfinch
```

a) blue head, blue wings, yellow front

_____

b) blue head, red front

_____

c) blue head, brown wings, cream front

_____

Understanding Science | Schofield & Sims   Animals and Plants 15

Habitats

The place where an organism lives is its **habitat**. A habitat can contain lots of different **organisms**, and it can be very big or very small.

This field is a large habitat.

The hedge is a smaller habitat.

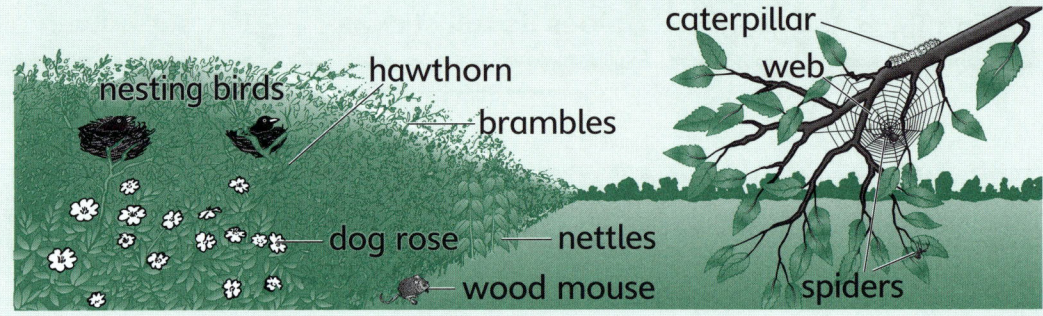

The soil under a stone is a very small habitat.

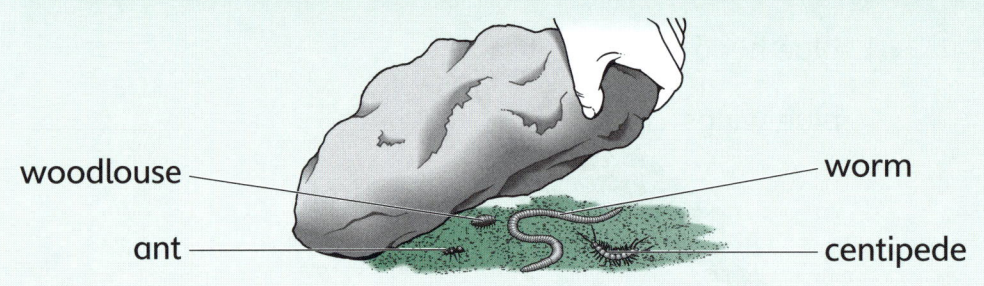

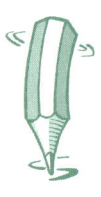

1. a) Write down four plants that live in a field habitat.

_____

b) Write down four animals that live in a field habitat.

_____

2. Complete this table to show what lives in the hedge habitat.

Plants	Animals

16 Animals and Plants   Schofield & Sims | Understanding Science

Habitats

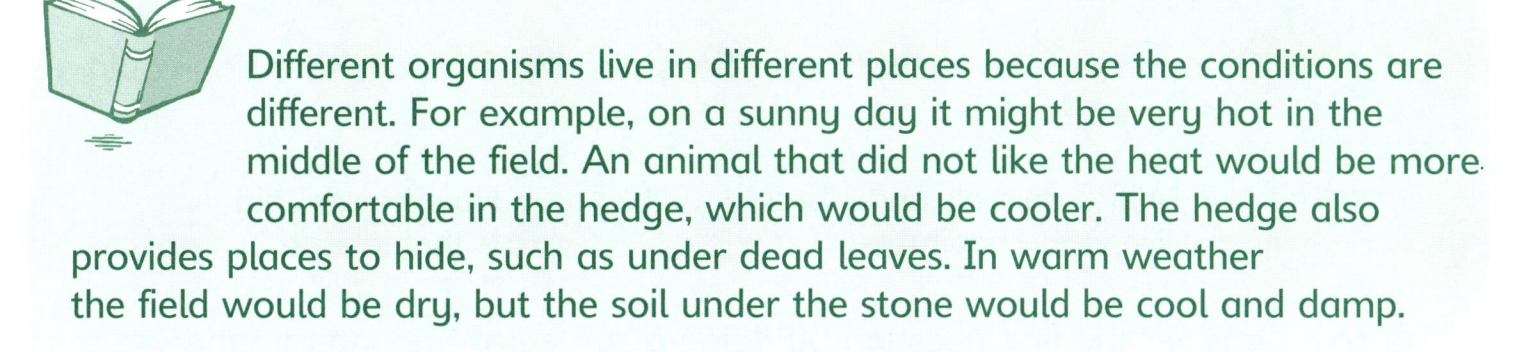

Different organisms live in different places because the conditions are different. For example, on a sunny day it might be very hot in the middle of the field. An animal that did not like the heat would be more comfortable in the hedge, which would be cooler. The hedge also provides places to hide, such as under dead leaves. In warm weather the field would be dry, but the soil under the stone would be cool and damp.

3. The table shows the conditions in the three different habitats on a hot day. Fill in the table using words from the box. You can use some words more than once.

Field	In the hedge	Under a stone

cool   damp   dark   dry   hot   light
shady   sheltered   warm   windy

4. A millipede likes to hide under dead leaves. Which of the habitats on this page might it live in? _____

5. Why are there no plants growing in the habitat under the stone? If you need a clue, look back to page 12 to remind yourself what plants need to grow.

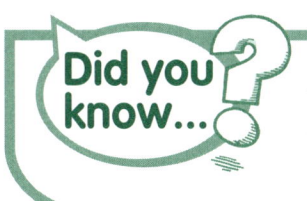

Did you know... An animal can be a habitat! Fleas are tiny insects that live in the fur of animals and feed on their blood.

Investigating habitats

There are lots of scientific questions about a **habitat** that you could investigate, such as:

> Which animals and plants live in the habitat?

> How hot or cold is the habitat?

You could answer the first question by doing a survey of the habitat, and use a **key** to identify the animals and plants there. You could answer the second one by measuring the temperature.

There are other questions that are a bit harder to investigate, such as:

> Why do woodlice live under stones?

You need to think of some possible reasons why they might live there, such as finding food there, or liking the dark, damp conditions. You can carry out an experiment to find out if woodlice really do like dark and damp conditions.

This is a choice chamber.

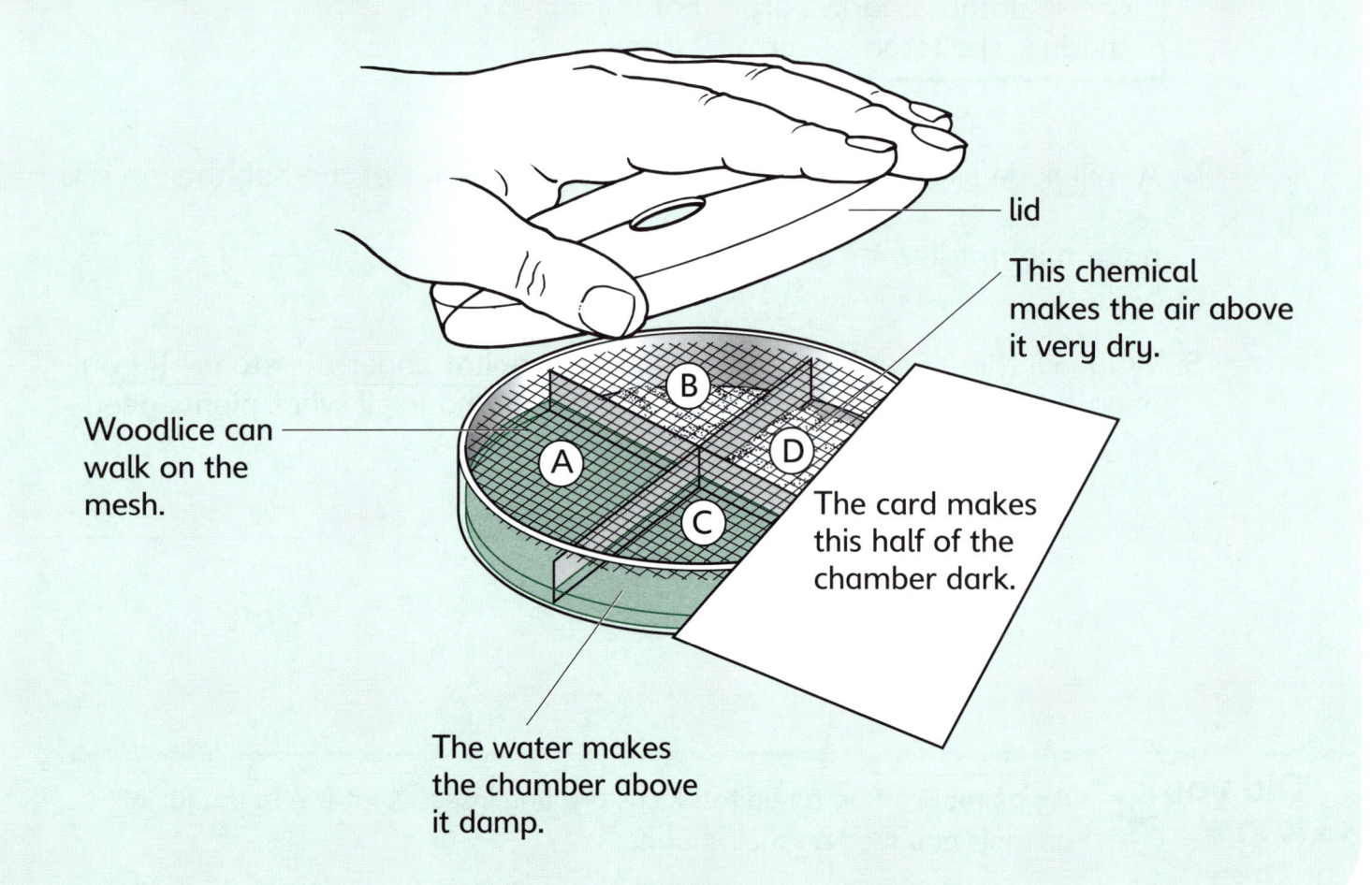

- lid
- This chemical makes the air above it very dry.
- Woodlice can walk on the mesh.
- The card makes this half of the chamber dark.
- The water makes the chamber above it damp.

18 Animals and Plants

Schofield & Sims | Understanding Science

Investigating habitats

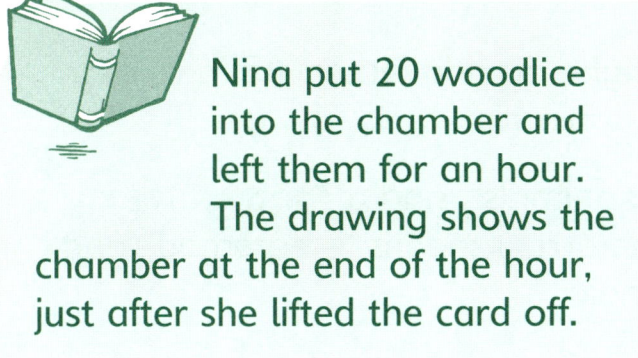

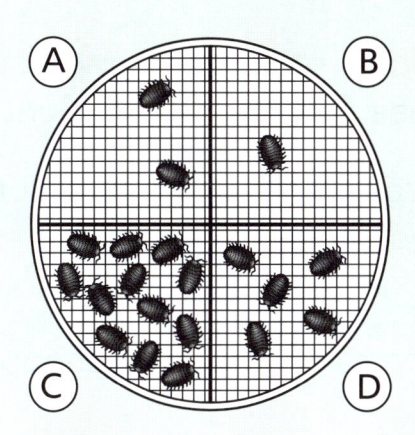

Nina put 20 woodlice into the chamber and left them for an hour. The drawing shows the chamber at the end of the hour, just after she lifted the card off.

1. Complete the table to show Nina's results.

Section	Conditions	Number of woodlice
A	light and damp	
B		
C		
D	dark and dry	

2. a) Which conditions do the woodlice prefer? _____

   b) Explain how you worked out your answer.

   _____

3. Why do you think that Nina used 20 woodlice instead of just one?

   _____

   _____

4. Nina wants to find out what woodlice eat. What should she do?

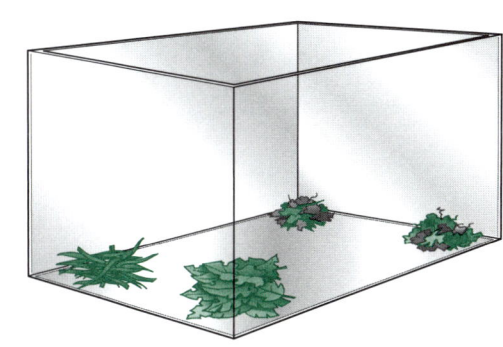

   _____

   _____

   _____

Food chains

Plants make their own food using light, air and water. Animals get their food by eating plants or other animals.

We can show the food for different animals using a **food chain**. This is a food chain for a garden **habitat**. The arrow means 'is eaten by', and shows the way that food goes through the chain.

grass → grasshopper → frog → heron

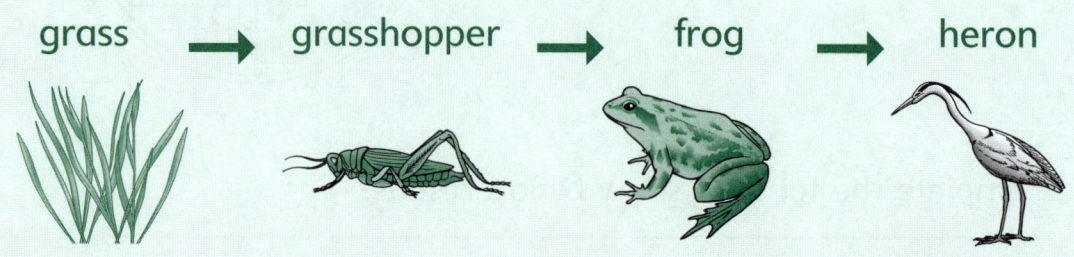

A food chain always starts with a plant. Plants are called **producers**, because they produce their own food. Animals are **consumers**, because they consume (eat) food made by plants.

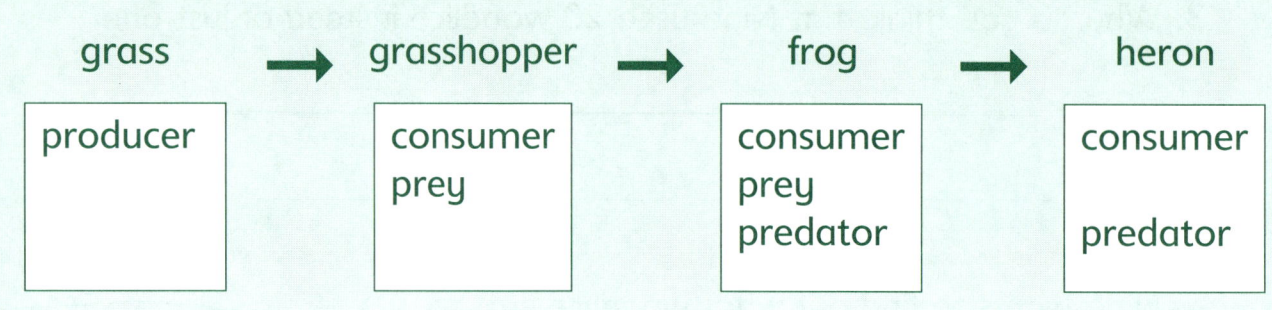

1. a) Which is the producer in the food chain above? _____

b) Which are the consumers?

_____

Predators are animals that eat other animals. The animals a predator eats are called its **prey**. The boxes show the words that can be used to describe the different parts of the food chain.

grass → grasshopper → frog → heron

grass	grasshopper	frog	heron
producer	consumer prey	consumer prey predator	consumer predator

20 Animals and Plants

Food chains

2. a) Why is the grasshopper called a consumer?

_____

b) Why is it called prey? _____

3. Why is the heron called a predator? _____

4. a) Why is the frog called prey? _____

b) Why is it called a predator? _____

This is another food chain from a garden habitat.

lettuce → snail → thrush → sparrowhawk

The snail is a **herbivore** because it only eats plants.

The sparrowhawk is a **carnivore**, because it only eats other animals.

A thrush likes to eat berries and seeds as well as snails and worms. It is an **omnivore**, because it eats food from both animals and plants.

5. Which organisms in the food chain are:

a) predators? _____

b) prey? _____

6. Use the facts in the box to help you to write a food chain.

> Foxes are predators.
> Lettuce is a producer.
> Rabbits are herbivores.

_____

Adaptations

Organisms are **adapted** to the places where they live. This means that they have features that help them to survive there.

A fox eats rabbits and other animals. It has sharp teeth to kill and tear up its **prey**. It can run fast to catch its prey.

A rabbit's teeth help it to grind up grass. Rabbits have strong back legs to help them to run away from **predators**, and ears to help them to hear when predators are coming.

This drawing shows a pond **habitat**.

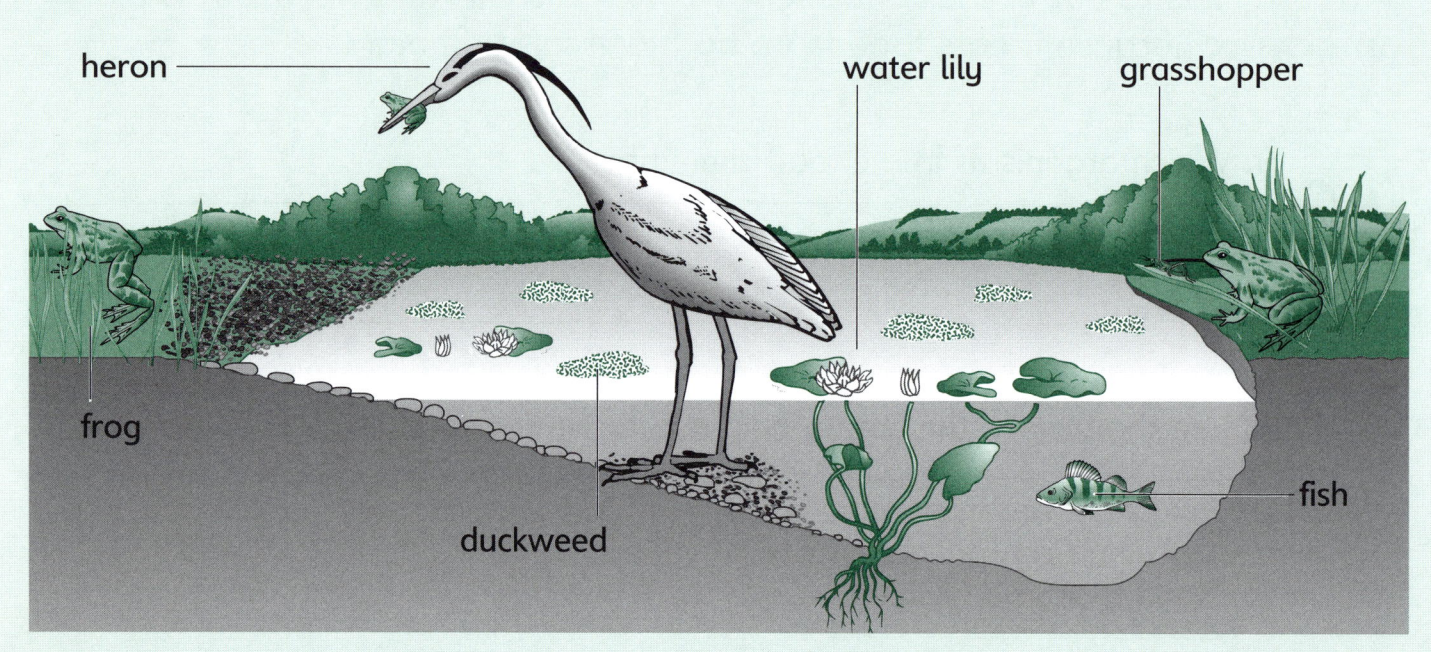

- heron
- water lily
- grasshopper
- frog
- duckweed
- fish

Fish are adapted to living in water. They have gills to help them to breathe underwater, and they have fins to help them to swim.

Adaptations

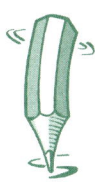

1. a) How is the heron adapted to living near water?

   _____

   b) How is the heron adapted to catching its prey?

   _____

2. Plants need light to grow well.

   a) How is a water lily adapted to living in water?

   _____

   b) How is duckweed adapted to living in water?

   _____

3. a) How is a frog adapted to help it to escape from predators?

   _____

   b) How is a frog adapted to catching its prey?

   _____

4. Write the correct words from the box next to each organism. You need to write more than one word for some of the organisms. (You might need to look back at pages 20 and 21.)

   frog   _____

   heron   _____

   water lily   _____

   | consumer   predator |
   | prey   producer |

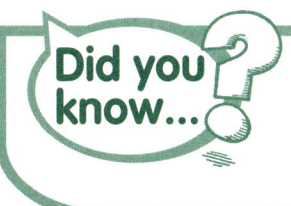

Did you know... Some habitats are very cold in winter, and there is no food around. Some animals adapt to the cold by hibernating, which is a bit like going to sleep for the whole winter.

Changing habitats

Animals in a **habitat** depend on plants for food, but they also need plants for shelter or to help to make their homes. Many animals also depend on other animals for food.

- many birds make their nest in trees
- woodpeckers eat insects that live under the bark on trees
- cows use the tree for shade on sunny days
- hedgehogs make nests using grass and fallen leaves

Many plants depend on animals. Some plants need insects to spread their pollen, and some plants need animals to spread their seeds. Animal droppings add fertiliser to the soil, which helps plants to grow.

1. How do these animals depend on the trees in the drawing above?

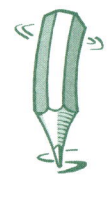

   a) cows _____

   b) hedgehogs _____

   c) woodpeckers _____

24 Animals and Plants   Schofield & Sims | Understanding Science

Changing habitats

Because many things in a habitat depend on each other, changing one part of a habitat can affect many **organisms**. If the trees in the drawing are cut down, the insects living in the bark may die, or will have to find another tree to live in. The woodpecker will have to find its food somewhere else, and the birds will have to find other trees for their nests.

Humans often change habitats. For example, gardeners may clear water weed from their ponds, or use 'slug pellets' to kill slugs and snails.

2. This is a food chain in Mrs Marshall's pond:

water weed → tadpole → perch → pike

What will happen if Mrs Marshall removes the water weed from her pond?

_____

_____

3. This is a food chain in Mr Smith's garden:

lettuce → snail → thrush → sparrowhawk

a) Why would Mr Smith want to kill the snails? _____

_____

b) What will happen to the thrushes if all the snails are killed? _____

_____

c) What will happen to the lettuce plants? _____

_____

Understanding Science | Schofield & Sims   Animals and Plants   **25**

Micro-organisms and decay

Food goes mouldy and rotten if you leave it out for too long. This happens because tiny living **organisms** called mould have grown on it and made it **decay**.

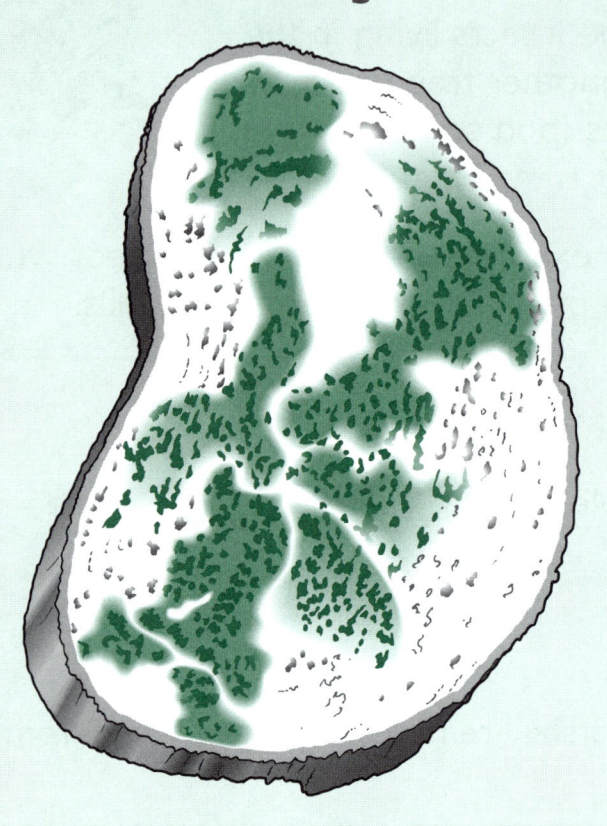

There are many different organisms that can make food or other materials decay. Most of these organisms are too small to see. They are called **micro-organisms** (or microbes). The micro-organisms feed on the food, and this is what makes it decay. These micro-organisms can make you ill if you eat food that they have been growing on.

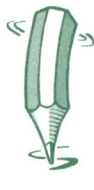

1. What makes decay happen?

   _____

2. What can happen if you eat decaying food?

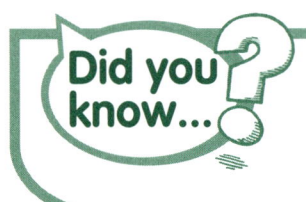

   _____

Did you know... Some micro-organisms do not need to eat dead plants or animals. They can get the energy they need from chemicals in rock or deep in the sea.

26 Animals and Plants   Schofield & Sims | Understanding Science

Micro-organisms and decay

When plants die, micro-organisms use them for food and the dead leaves or stems rot away. When an animal dies, its body is sometimes eaten by other animals. Any remains that are left will decay.

Decay is useful because it puts **nutrients** into the soil. Plants take nutrients out of the soil when they grow, and the nutrients end up in the leaves or stems. When the plant dies, decay allows the nutrients to go back into the soil so they can be used by other plants. If decay did not happen, the soil would run out of nutrients and plants would not be able to grow there.

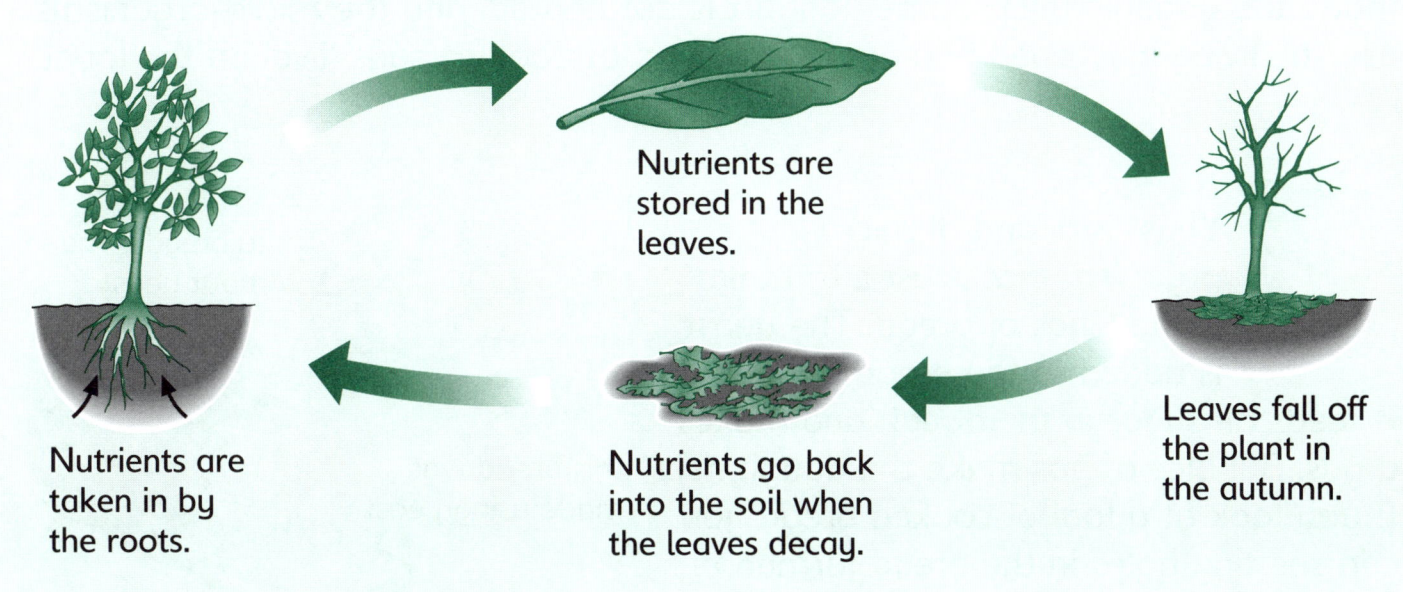

Nutrients are stored in the leaves.

Leaves fall off the plant in the autumn.

Nutrients go back into the soil when the leaves decay.

Nutrients are taken in by the roots.

Decay can help us to get rid of some of our rubbish. Materials like paper and wood decay if they are left long enough. Other materials like plastic, metal and glass do not decay.

3. What would happen to dead plants if decay did not happen?

_____

4. a) What is a nutrient? _____

b) How does decay add nutrients to the soil?

_____

_____

Using micro-organisms

Micro-organisms are very useful in making all the foods shown here.

Yoghurt is made from milk. The milk is heated first, to kill any micro-organisms in it that might make you ill. Then special micro-organisms are added. These feed on the milk and make it thicker.

The yoghurt can be heated again to kill the micro-organisms after they have made the yoghurt thick. Some yoghurt is not heated, and the micro-organisms are still living in it when you eat it! This kind of yoghurt says 'live' on the label.

Yeast is a kind of micro-organism that is used to make some kinds of bread. The yeast is added to the bread dough. It feeds on sugar in the dough and makes a gas. Bubbles of gas make the dough rise. If you look at a loaf of cooked bread you can see tiny holes in the bread formed by bubbles of gas.

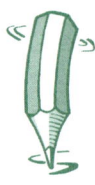

1. Write down four foods that are made using micro-organisms.

   _____

2. How do micro-organisms make yoghurt from milk?

   _____

3. What does yeast do when bread is made?

   _____

   _____

4. Why is pitta bread very flat? _____

Using micro-organisms

Like other **organisms**, yeast is alive. It needs food and warmth to make it grow and reproduce. Ollie wanted to show that yeast is a living organism. He set up some tubes like this:

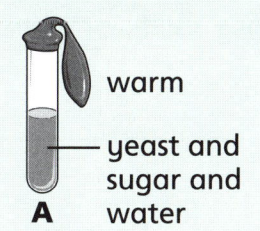

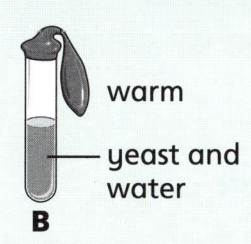

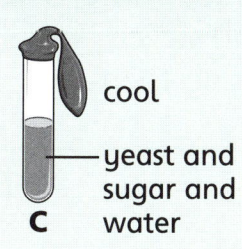

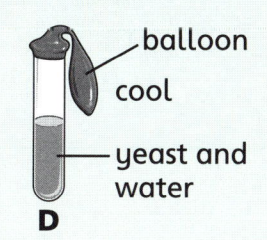

A — warm — yeast and sugar and water
B — warm — yeast and water
C — cool — yeast and sugar and water
D — cool — yeast and water (balloon)

After a few hours, one of Ollie's tubes looked like this:

This shows that the yeast in the tube has been growing and making gas.

5. a) Which tube do you think contained the yeast that was making gas?

_____

b) Why do you think it was this tube?

_____

_____

6. Complete these sentences to explain why the yeast in the other tubes did not grow.

The yeast in tube ____ did not grow because _____

_____.

The yeast in tube ____ did not grow because _____

_____.

The yeast in tube ____ did not grow because _____

_____.

Scientific investigation

In this book you have found out about animals and plants and how they live and depend on each other. You have also learnt how to investigate some scientific questions. Good scientists need many different skills in order to investigate things. You can learn some of the other skills you need in the other **Understanding Science** books. The table below shows you the skills you need, and which books help to teach you these skills or give you practice in using them.

Skill	Book pages					
	Animals and Plants	Our Bodies	Using Materials	Changing Materials	Forces and Electricity	Light, Sound and Space
Planning an investigation						
Asking a scientific question			10		6	
Knowing what factors are	6–7			8, 22, 24		6–7
Planning a fair test	6–7		10–11, 20–21	8–9	6–7, 12	6–7, 16
Predicting what you think you will find out		28–29	17		6–7	16
Recording and presenting your evidence						
Making tally charts		27				
Drawing pictograms		8				
Drawing bar charts		8, 27	12–13, 20	22–23, 24–25		
Drawing line graphs		28–29		10, 22–23, 24–25		6–7
Considering your evidence and evaluating it						
Writing a conclusion	6–7	9	12–13, 20	9, 10, 25	7, 13	
Evaluating your investigation	6–7	9, 26	13	9, 10	13	17

Answers

Page 4

1. roots – take in water, hold the plant in the soil
   leaves – make food
   stem – supports the plant, carries water to the leaves
   flowers – help the plant to reproduce

2. roots, stem, leaves

Page 5

1. pollen and ovum (egg)

2. growth, flower formed, pollination, fertilisation, seed formed, dispersal, germination

Pages 6 and 7

1. a) the amount of water
   b) the number of seedlings, the warmth and the amount of light

2. The seedlings grew best when they had some water.

3. The plants did not grow properly in the dish with no light, but they did grow in the dish that was left in the light.

4. The only factor that Liam changed was the amount of light (**or**, Liam kept the temperature and the amount of water the same).

5. The plants will grow best in the dish that was left in the warm.

6. The investigation was a fair test. Liam used a lot of plants because plants are different and one may not have grown well anyway.

Pages 8 and 9

1.

Parts of flower	What they do
sepals	protect the petals when they are in a bud
stamens	produce pollen
petals	attract insects
ovary	grows into a fruit when the ovum has been fertilised
stigma	sticky, so pollen grains stick to it
ovum	grows into a seed when it has been fertilised

2. to attract insects to the flower

3. by the wind

4. 3 The insect visits a different flower.
   5 A tube grows down the stigma.
   1 The stamens make pollen.
   2 An insect visits the flower to drink nectar, and some pollen sticks to it.
   4 Pollen from the insect sticks to the stigma.
   6 An ovum is fertilised and grows into a seed.

Understanding Science | Schofield & Sims   Animals and Plants   31

Answers

Page 10
1. so the new plants have space to grow (**or** so the new plants have enough light, air and water)

2. a) by sticking to an animal's fur
   b) They eat them, and the seeds come out in their droppings.

3. a) by the wind
   b) The wind will blow them easily because they are fluffy (**or**, other fluffy seeds are dispersed by the wind).

Page 11
1. The seeds germinated in the dish even though it did not have any light.

2. B

3. Seeds need warmth to germinate.

4. to check that there was nothing wrong with the seeds and that they did germinate when they had the right conditions

5. a) no
   b) The seeds in dishes A and D germinated, and they were not in soil.

6. water, warmth

Page 12
1. leaves

2. through the roots

3. substances that plants need to grow well

4. through the roots

5. a) All plants need water to grow.
   b) Some plants can grow in very dry conditions, so they do not need 'lots' of water.

Page 13
1. any two from: provide a home, provide clothes, provide food, take me to school, play with me, buy me toys

2. You could have written down some of these things: eat, drink, walk, get dressed, wash, go to the toilet.

3. any two differences such as: ducks lay eggs but humans have babies; ducks lay lots of eggs at once, humans usually have only one baby at a time; ducks can have their own babies after only a year, it takes humans much longer

Answers

Pages 14 and 15

1. animal, vertebrate
2. plant
3. a) blue tit
   b) chaffinch
   c) sparrow

Pages 16 and 17

1. a) any four from: grass, thistle, buttercup, clover, oak tree
   b) rabbit, song thrush, grasshopper, spider – You could also have put cows, horses, sheep or pigs.

2.

Plants	Animals
hawthorn	wood mouse
nettles	birds
brambles	spiders
dog rose	caterpillar

3.

Field	In the hedge	Under a stone
light	shady	dark
hot	warm	cool
dry	damp or dry	damp
windy	sheltered	sheltered

4. in the hedge
5. There is no light, and plants need light to grow.

Pages 18 and 19

1.

Section	Conditions	Number of woodlice
A	light and damp	2
B	light and dry	1
C	dark and damp	12
D	dark and dry	5

2. a) dark and damp
   b) Most of the woodlice were in the dark and damp part of the chamber.

3. Not all woodlice are the same, so one by itself might have liked light or dry conditions.

Understanding Science | Schofield & Sims   Animals and Plants **33**

Answers

        4. She could put some woodlice in a container and put different kinds of food in different places. She should watch them to see which food most of them move towards or eat.

Pages 20 and 21

1. a) grass
   b) grasshopper, frog, heron

2. a) It eats plants for food.
   b) It gets eaten by frogs.

3. It eats frogs (**or** It eats other animals).

4. a) It gets eaten by herons.
   b) It eats grasshoppers.

5. a) thrush, sparrowhawk
   b) snail, thrush

6. lettuce → rabbit → fox

Pages 22 and 23

1. a) It has long legs.
   b) It has a long beak.

2. a) It has long stems and floating leaves, so the leaves can get light.
   b) It floats, so the leaves can get light.

3. a) It has long legs to help it to jump.
   b) It has a long tongue.

4. frog: consumer, predator, prey
   heron: consumer, predator
   water lily: producer

Pages 24 and 25

1. a) They need the trees for shade.
   b) They need the dead leaves for their nests.
   c) They feed on the insects that live in the bark.

2. The tadpoles will have nothing to eat and will die. The perch and pike will have no food, so they will die too.

3. a) They eat the plants in his garden.
   b) They will have no food, so they might die or they might move to another garden.
   c) They will grow better, because the snails are not eating them.

Pages 26 and 27

1. micro-organisms feeding on food

2. You can be ill.

3. They would pile up and get in the way.

Answers

    4. a) a substance that plants need to help them to grow well
       b) Nutrients used by plants stay in their leaves or stems. Nutrients go back into the soil when the plant dies and decays.

Pages 28 and 29

1. any four from: bread, cheese, yoghurt, Marmite, wine, beer, Quorn
2. They make the milk go thick.
3. It makes gas bubbles, which makes the bread rise.
4. It has no yeast in the dough to make gas.
5. **a)** A
   b) This tube has sugar (food) and it was kept warm.
6. The yeast in tube B did not grow because there was no sugar (food).
   The yeast in tube C did not grow because it was too cold (or it was not warm enough).
   The yeast in tube D did not grow because there was no sugar (food) and it was too cold (or it was not warm enough).

Index and glossary

adapted 12, 22	having features to help it to survive
carnivore 21	an animal that eats only other animals
conclusion 6	what you have found out in an investigation
consumers 20	animals that eat plants or other animals
decay 26	what happens when **micro-organisms** feed on dead **organisms**
dispersed 5, 10	spread out, as when seeds are dispersed from the parent plant
evaluation 7	where you say how good your investigation was and whether it was a fair test
factor 6	the things that you could change in an investigation
fertilisation 5, 9	when a pollen grain joins an ovum in a flower
food chain 20, 25	a way of showing what eats what
germination 5, 11	when seeds start to grow
habitat 16, 18, 20, 22, 24	the place where an organism lives
herbivore 21	an animal that only eats plants
invertebrates 14	animals that don't have a backbone
key 14, 18	a set of questions to help us to identify different **organisms**
life cycle 5, 13	all the changes that happen to animals or plants as they get older and **reproduce**
micro-organisms 26, 28	tiny **organisms**, sometimes called microbes
nutrients 12, 27	substances that a plant needs small amounts of to keep healthy and grow well
omnivore 21	an animal that eats plants and other animals
organisms 14, 16, 22, 25, 26, 29	any kind of living thing is an organism
pollination 5, 8	when pollen from one flower is taken to another flower
predators 20, 22	animals that kill other animals for food
prey 20, 22	an animal that gets eaten by other animals
producers 20	plants – all plants produce their own food from water, air and light
reproduce 4, 5, 8	to make a new animal or plant
vertebrates 14	animals that have a backbone (humans are vertebrates)